I thought I knew how to
Google

I thought I knew how to

50 tricks for refining your search

Miha Mazzini

Translated by Lučka Lučovnik

An Imprint of HarperCollins *Publishers*

First published in India in 2012 by Collins
an imprint of HarperCollins *Publishers* India
a joint venture with
The India Today Group

First published in Slovene in 2009 as Mislilsem, da obvladam Google

Copyright © Založba Rokus Klett (Ljubljana 2009).
Authorized translation from the Slovene-language edition
published by Založba Rokus Klett

ISBN: 978-93-5029-231-0

2 4 6 8 10 9 7 5 3 1

Miha Mazzini asserts the moral right to be identified
as the author of this book.

Photo credits: 13: SHT (Lars Christensen); 16: SHT (Sebastian Kaulitzki); 17: WC; 18: SHT (James Steidl); 19: WC; 21: WC; 22: SHT (Tatiana Popova); 23: SHT (Len Green); 26–27: IST (GlobalP); 29: IST (pixhook); 30: SHT (BlueOrange Studio); 32: SHT (Hoomar); 34: SHT (Mikael Damkier). SHT – Shutterstock; IST – iStockphoto; WC – Wikimedia Commons

The views expressed in this book are those of the author and do not reflect the views of Google Inc. or any of its subsidiaries or affiliated companies

All rights reserved. No part of this publication may be reproduced, stored in a retrieval system, or transmitted, in any form or by any means, electronic, mechanical, photocopying, recording or otherwise, without the prior permission of the publishers.

HarperCollins *Publishers*
A-53, Sector 57, NOIDA, Uttar Pradesh – 201301, India
77-85 Fulham Palace Road, London W6 8JB, United Kingdom
Hazelton Lanes, 55 Avenue Road, Suite 2900, Toronto, Ontario M5R 3L2
and 1995 Markham Road, Scarborough, Ontario M1B 5M8, Canada
25 Ryde Road, Pymble, Sydney, NSW 2073, Australia
31 View Road, Glenfield, Auckland 10, New Zealand
10 East 53rd Street, New York NY 10022, USA

Text design: **Aleš Pučnik**
Typeset in 10/12 Humanist 521 BT
Jojy Philip New Delhi 110 015

Printed and bound at
Thomson Press (India) Ltd.

Contents

Introduction	3
A quick glance at the internet	4
The basics of googling	8
First time on Google?	8
Choosing the language	10
Anatomy of the Google page	11
Choice of search string	13
Results: the less the better	14
1. Words you want to include	15
2. Words you want to exclude	16
3. When you can't decide	17
4. Searching for an exact word or phrase	18
5. Combining commands	19
6. Search within a specific website	20
7. Searching within a domain	21
8. Searching for related sites	22
9. Searching for synonyms	23
10. Searching for any word	24
11. Searching for numbers	25
12. Searching only within website titles	26
13. Searching within titles and content of websites	27
14. Searching within the web address	28
15. Searching within the web address and content	29
16. Basic image search	30
17. Searching within certain file formats	31
18. Is this site still active?	33
Everyday information	34
19. Calculator	35
20. Converting units of measure	37

21. Converting numbers	38
22. Converting currency	39
23. Constants	40
24. The meaning of life	41
25. Explanations from dictionaries and encyclopaedias	42
26. What's the time?	43
27. What's the weather like?	44
28. Music	45
29. Movies	46
30. Easter eggs	47
31. Searching for flights	48
32. Birthdays and birthplaces	49
33. Stocks	50
34. Where's that country, anyway?	51
35. And where is this city?	52
36. The highest mountains	53
37. Number of inhabitants in a country	54
38. Capitals	55
39. GDP	56
40. Radius of planets	57
41. Masses of planets	58
Advanced search	59
42. The advanced search form	60
Translation from foreign languages	63
43. Searching through websites in a foreign language	65
44. Translating text	66
45. Translating websites	67
Google's topic-specific search	68
46. Map search	71
47. Image search	75
48. Searching through blogs	76
49. Alerts	80
50. What do others search for?	82

I thought I knew how to

Google

Introduction

In the past, whenever I mentioned that I was writing a book of instructions on how to use Google, everybody would start to laugh: Why write about something we all know?
But do we really know all?
Google hides many useful things that have never been heard of by most users. I was delighted to hear the "oohs" and "aahs" and similar expressions of astonishment from the test readers of the book you are holding in your hands.
I'll tell it as it is: if your internet search isn't effective, you're wasting time and energy, and your results are far from perfect.
I could have written a comprehensive book on Google – but I didn't want to do that. I decided to gather all the tricks and tips that I find most useful. However, you have to recognize that Google is changing quickly and new possibilities are being added constantly. I can only say that when this book was published, Google was just as it says here.
By searching on Google, you can't cause damage to the World Wide Web, or to your computer, so don't be afraid and just start searching!

A quick glance at the internet

Google is a search engine that searches through websites. If you *really* know what that means, you can easily skip through this chapter.

Website
A website is a document designed to be shown on the internet. It can consist of a text, pictures, video clips, etc.
Websites are written in a special code language called HTML, and that is why their names usually end with .HTML or .HTM.

Web address
Each website has its own address, which makes it easily accessible. Example: www.wikipedia.org.
Some web addresses are called domains or URLs
(Uniform Resource Locators)

Browser and Toolbars
In order to see websites, you need a special program called a browser. Firefox, Microsoft Internet Explorer and Google Chrome are among the most commonly known ones.
Each browser can have one or more toolbars – a series of icons giving orders and showing empty boxes for you to find the text that you are searching for.

The computer system administrators assured me that many users aren't able to tell the difference between a web address, a toolbar and a website, so they type words anywhere. There is no need for that – you will be much more efficient if you know how to enter a web address and a search string in the correct boxes.

A title bar for a web address (your way of telling the browser which website you want)

A toolbar for a search string (a browser may or may not contain this box; if it does, you can type a search string into it)

An open Google website, which also requires a search string

Website title

Do not mix up the address of a website (to a browser, this is like a postal address to a postman – directions to where he has to go) with the title of a website (this is something like the title of an article or book – an inscription that appears in the browser's frame, so that you, the user, know where you are).

This is a website title.

And this is a website address.

Directories

No one can remember the addresses of all websites. That's why there are lists of websites, arranged according to their content. In these directories, people can add information about websites they would like to make public. An example of such a directory list is Dmoz: www.dmoz.org.

Search engines and Spiders
Since browsing through directory lists is time-consuming too, there are now search engines. Although the data about websites in directory lists is managed by people, the search engine has a program called a spider that constantly travels around the internet, picking up content from websites and arranging them into a huge index. To simplify: you get a table of each keyword and the websites where the spider found them.

Searching, a Search String and Hits
Type in one or more keywords (a search string) and the search engine will check its site index and give you a list of all the sites that contain that keyword. The pages found by the spider are called hits.

Google
Google is currently the leading search engine; it is found on the web address www.google.co.in.

Googling
In 2006, a new verb appeared in leading English dictionaries: to google. It denotes searching on the web with the help of the search engine Google.

The basics of googling

First time on Google?

The Google web address is: www.google.co.in.

Type www.google.co.in in the title bar of your browser and press the ENTER key.

You will see a typical page, bereft of all that's unnecessary – there's space in the middle for you to type in a search string. In short, that's a really **basic search**.

Type in a search keyword, i.e. aspirin.

Click this key and the search will begin.

Google offers you a list of hits.

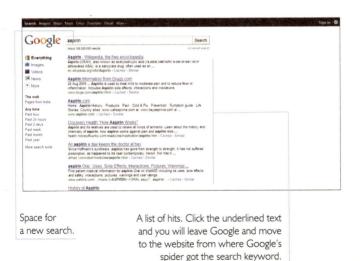

Space for a new search.

A list of hits. Click the underlined text and you will leave Google and move to the website from where Google's spider got the search keyword.

Choosing the language

Google (www.google.co.in) is, of course, in English. However, you can choose a language you want to read on the screen, regardless of which page you are on. Let's see how you can switch to Hindi from the English Google.

Click the link Hindi.

Google also teaches you how to search in your preferred language.

Anatomy of the Google page

A natural human need for decoration becomes most obvious with Christmas trees and with websites – website authors often add anything they possibly can. The more, the better. Well, this is not true for a user, who can quickly get lost in the middle of all that rubbish. Since its very beginning, Google has been striving to add as little as possible to the page, but still the screen is full of links that you may find useful.

1 You can decide where to search (Search, Images, News, Maps, etc.) or which Google services to use (Gmail, Calendar, Photos, Documents, Sites). In this book, only the first group of links will be presented, because this group is important in order to get good hits.

2 You can sign in and adjust Google to your wishes.

3 You can enter your search string – keywords that relate to what you are looking for (page 14).

The "I'm feeling Lucky" key takes you directly to the web page that's first on the list (it skips the list).

A key that starts searching and writes out a list of hits.

Two very important links that we will be talking about often: "Advanced Search" is explained on pages 59–62, and "Language Tools" is explained on pages 63–67.

4 Informative links at the bottom of the page.

Choice of search string

You can type in a single keyword, but you will probably get a huge number of hits, and that would take up a lot of your time. It's better to type in more keywords that best describe your search item:

goa travel air

The keyword you find the most important should come first, the rest should follow according to their importance (at least approximately – Google knows its way around even without your help). You can type in 32 words at most.
You can write with capital or small letters, you can even mix them up – it makes no difference to Google.
You can easily leave out some very common words: "I", "is", "the", and others.
In short, Google will search for pages that contain all three words.

Results: the less the better

Besides search strings, you can type commands in the Google search box – they determine Google's behaviour and tell it what to do. The commands are mathematical symbols (+, –) or full English words (OR, site:). Example:

+something –second third OR fourth

Don't panic, it's not complicated. Let's start at the beginning.

Words you want to include | 1

If a certain word is extremely important and you want each search result to contain it, preface it with a plus (+) symbol, without leaving a space in between. In the following example, the airplane is essential:

```
goa travel +air
```

Attention: Remember to preface the plus symbol (an additional command for Google for the word "air") with a single space!

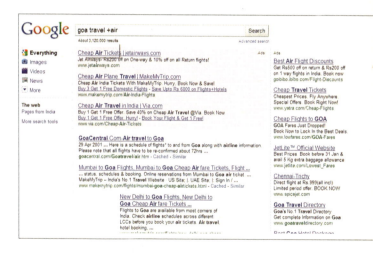

2 | Words you want to exclude

Sometimes you need to search for a word that has more than one meaning or you want to exclude sites that contain a particular word. Preface that word with a minus (–) symbol, again with no space in between. Are you afraid of flying? Then you definitely don't want to travel by plane! Therefore, you are not interested in sites containing the word air:

> **goa travel –air**

Suppose you want information on viruses. As you know, the same word stands for a computer virus and for an infectious agent. If you are only interested in the last, type this:

> **virus –computer**

As you can see, there is a space prefacing the minus symbol.

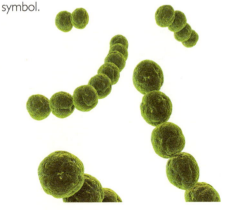

When you can't decide | 3

Sometimes you would like to get a list of hits relating to either one or another word. In that case, you put OR between the two keywords. Let's say you want to travel but you don't care whether you fly to Goa or Mumbai:

```
goa OR mumbai travel air
```

Attention: The OR command has to be typed with capital letters!
The symbol | can stand for OR, but it's difficult to find this symbol on every keyboard:

```
goa | mumbai travel air
```

You can merge keywords with brackets and make logical expressions:

```
travel (goa OR mumbai) (air OR train)
```

4 | Searching for an exact word or phrase

If you type in several keywords, Google will try to find the best possible hits. However, sometimes you will want to tell Google to search for an exact phrase, exactly as you typed it in the search box. In that case, put quotation marks (" ") at the beginning and the end of the query:

"brothers in arms"

Quotation marks come in handy when searching for kings, too:

"henry viii"

Or when searching for a program:

"windows 7"

Combining commands | 5

The plus and minus symbols and quotation marks can easily be combined, which helps you customize your search. In the following example we want to find Zeppelin, but not the airship nor the car – the band. So you type:

zeppelin –airship –car +band

If you are interested in the airship, just type:

zeppelin +airship –car –band

6 Searching within a specific website

Some websites don't have the option of searching through their content, some have insufficient options and sometimes you don't feel like opening the site and you would like Google to check if the query exists on a certain site. You have to know the web address and preface it with the site: command.

Attention: the word site and a colon, followed directly by a web address!

Let's say HarperCollins has published a book on dieting:

"diet book" site:www.harpercollins.co.in

It often happens that you need contact information on employees of a certain company, which is sometimes very well hidden. Try searching this way:

contact site:www.ngmaindia.gov.in

When searching for a person with a profile on Facebook, the top results will be from this site. You can omit the results from this site by combining the commands minus (–) and site:

john doe –site:www.facebook.com

Searching within a domain | 7

The site: command can be used for searching within web addresses of only certain countries. The .in ending is for Indian domains; therefore, you can write:

```
car site:.in
```

Google will search for the word car on all websites with the domain ending in .in.
One of the important endings is .edu, which is owned by most educational institutions – that way, you can narrow down your search results to suit your purpose.

```
darwin site:.edu
```

8 | Searching for related sites

There are huge numbers of websites, and yes, Google has visited more of them than you will ever be able to. Google has also read them thoroughly, which means it can make conclusions on their details. The related: command tells Google to suggest similar websites to the one you suggested. Example:

related:www.hindustantimes.com

That's a newspaper website and Google does a good job recommending another newspaper's website www.indianexpress.com as the first choice (this was true during the time this handbook was published). This command can be of great help when you finally reach the website on the topic you want to find out more about, as you can then demand related sites.

Searching for synonyms | 9

Attention: This command does not yet work with words in languages other than English!

Let's say you are searching for English automobile sites. You type in the word "car". But what if the author used another expression – vehicle, for example. These sites will not turn up among the hits. English Google can use a dictionary of synonyms. You can demand to find synonyms of the keyword.

You have to type in the ~ sign (tilde) in front of the keyword:

```
~car
```

On the list, you suddenly see "vehicle", "automotive", "racing", and so on. In short, the number of hits multiplies. This only means that you have to use other commands to narrow down your results. That's how you exclude all the BMW cars:

```
~car –bmw
```

10 Searching for any word

Hmm, this sounds like an extremely silly title, doesn't it? But then again…

Google knows the * command (asterisk), which tells it to consider any word or more words instead of this command.

Let's say you are doing your homework and you need to write down titles of all the works of Ernest Hemingway. Somebody must have done that before and put the list on the web. So type in:

```
ernest hemingway wrote*
```

If you put the asterisk at the end of a search string, Google will think you typed in the beginning of a sentence and want its continuation. Therefore, it will first show you the hits where your search string is followed by other words, which is exactly what you need in this case.

You can also put the asterisk between keywords. If you search like this:

```
happy saturday
```

Google will first show you all the hits where the two keywords are written exactly as you typed them. But if you want to tell Google that there can be one or more words between "happy" and "saturday", then type this:

```
happy * saturday
```

Searching for numbers | 11

Sometimes you want to find something within a specific topic. Let's say you are interested in weights that weigh between 5 and 10 kg, neither lighter nor heavier. Use the .. command (two dots one after another) that tells Google to check on the website found whether there are numbers from 5 to 10 next to the search string. That's how you find a weight that you are interested in:

> weights 5..10

Hmm, and what's this:

> girl 20..30

You can search like this when you are buying something – simply add currency to the numbers:

> dvd player Rs 1000..Rs 5000

Or you can type in the title of a specific book and add price limitation:

> "pride and prejudice" Rs 80..Rs 500

Yes, of course – this command helps you find the most attractive prices! Yay!

12 | Searching only within website titles

The website that has what you need in the title is probably the right one. That's why Google has the allintitle: command which makes it search only within the titles that contain **all** of the keywords.
Let's use an example of a website that will teach you how to take care of a dog.
If you type in:

> dog care

you will get many hits. There will be considerably fewer hits overall and yet many more of them will be precise if Google only searches in website titles:

> allintitle:dog care

Searching within titles and content of websites 13

If you want to combine commands and find one keyword in the title and the other in the text, do this:

`intitle:dog labrador`

In this case, the word "dog" must appear in the title of the site (the intitle: command stands before that word) and "labrador" must appear somewhere in the text. No one forbids you to enter more words in the search box, determining which should appear in the title and which in the text.

`intitle:dog intitle:labrador black`

14 Searching within the web address

You can either search only for keywords in website titles (page 26) or only in web addresses – allinurl:.
The following search shows hits with both words – "Ernest" and "Hemingway" – in a web address.

> allinurl:"ernest hemingway"

You can be sure you have found a web address about Ernest Hemingway.
This command can also be combined with other commands, for example, with site:. The following search is based on looking for a subsite that includes the word "personal" and will probably direct you to the personal banking page at HSBC:

> allinurl:personal site:hsbc.com

Here is how to search for the news only on Indian sites (.co.in ending):

> allinurl:news site:.co.in

Searching within the web address and content | 15

If you want to combine searching within web address and text, add the inurl: command at the beginning:

inurl:"ernest hemingway" "the old man and the sea"

The keyword "Ernest Hemingway" has to appear in the web address, and "The Old Man and the Sea" anywhere within the site.
Here is how to search for this only on British sites:

inurl:"ernest hemingway" "the old man and the sea" site:.uk

16 | Basic image search

Besides the search string, you can type in the word images in the basic search and Google will show you some images at the top of the hit list; in this case, images of babies:

> images baby

Due to the fact that people like to see pictures and therefore often search for them, Google has prepared a special site only for images. Learn more on pages 71–75.

Searching within certain file formats | 17

This demands a little more computer knowledge. If you think your heart can't handle it, you can go ahead and skip this chapter.

On the web, you can find many files written in special formats and Google recognizes some of them. Until recently, Microsoft Word has been using the DOC format; presentations with the Power Point program are written in the PPT format; the PDF format is used for various official messages, manuals and similar texts designed for printing. Therefore, if you want to read business reports in the form of documents, you can use the filetype: command, followed by a format, in this case PDF:

> "business report" filetype:pdf

If you are searching for a manual for a particular model of telephone:

> manual n8 filetype:pdf

You have to make a presentation (PPT file) on sustainable development. Oh, you can bet somebody has done this before you. Why don't you snoop around a little?

> "sustainable development" filetype:ppt

Now you're probably thinking about the MP3 ending that is a standard for recorded music on the internet. You can find it on Google, too, but obviously people don't want to get into any legal trouble, therefore Google search doesn't support this format. Even so, you can still type in the following search string containing Mozart, mp3 and two strings that are always on the list sites.

+mozart +mp3 +"index of" +"last modified"

Is this site still active? 18

Google's spider wanders through websites and transports all the words into the site index. However, there are a lot of sites, billions of them, and the spider can't visit them every second – it only returns there every now and then.

In practice, this means that the author could have changed the site entirely, but Google still has the old site index. Then, when you start your search, Google finds keywords in the site index and offers a site, but the expected content is nowhere to be seen. In this case, some commands may come in handy. The first one is cache:, followed by a web address:

```
cache:www.bbc.co.uk
```

Google shows a site from the site index, not from real life, along with the date and time of the visit.
The info: command, followed by a web address shows information about the site from the site index:

```
info:www.bbc.co.uk
```

You will see a list of links enabling you to further research the sites, and the site as it was when entered in the site index.

Everyday information

You are sitting at your computer, switching among the calculator, maps, encyclopaedias, dictionaries, directories etc. Well, there's probably no need for that. Google can replace many programs and data sources.

Calculator 19

This often comes in handy. You have to make a quick calculation, and, admit it, you probably reach for complicated applications which you have probably even paid for (oh, dear!). Google has a way of calmly and effectively solving mathematical expressions, typed in as search strings.

```
156 + 234
```

Google says the sum is 390 (I've just checked my calculator).
You can also use functions like tangent:

```
tan (4)
```

or:

```
sin (90) / cos (45)
```

You can type in more demanding expressions:

```
((12 + 2) * 9) – (sqrt (10) ^ 4)
```

Or you can find out how much you saved by buying on sale (Attention: in this case use the of command):

```
45% of 245
```

Attention: Of course, a hero came along who created a calculator that does not really calculate anything – it only sends your data to Google. However, it is simpler to use because it looks like a real calculator. Check out www.soople.com/soople_intcalchome.php.

And where can you find a list of everything the calculator is capable of doing? On Google, of course! Search:

google calculator quick reference

Converting units of measure | 20

When I was trying to find a recipe for an American dessert, I stumbled across units that aren't in the metric system: 3 oz chocolate. This is what I discovered when I typed:

```
3 oz in g
```

Google explained that this is 85 g (naturally, I added 100 g to the recipe because I love chocolate).
If you would like to know the measure of an inch in cm:

```
inch in cm
```

You are reading news on a basketball player who is 7.1 feet high:

```
7.1 feet in cm
```

How much is 12 degrees Fahrenheit in Celsius:

```
12 f in c
```

And so on and so forth. Be sure to write in between the first and second unit.

21 | Converting numbers

You are standing at a monument that was built in MCMXVII. Oh my, Roman numerals – primary school. Google can handle them – this command converts Roman numerals in capitals into Arabic:

MCMXVII in arabic

That's how it does it the other way around:

1814 in roman

I mustn't forget the computer engineers who need to use the hexadecimal numeral system:

42 in hex

And don't get me started on the binary system:

42 in binary

Converting currency | 22

To Google, the conversion from one currency to another is not a novelty. It can easily switch between currencies if you type in this:

```
16 gbp in eur
```

You will find out what 16 British pounds is in euros. Use the in command again and type in currencies instead of units:

```
16 eur in usd
```

```
300 yen in usd
```

```
1 eur in inr
```

23 | Constants

Google also knows some constants from mathematics and physics. Usually you just have to type in the name of a constant and Google will give you the numbers. Pi:

> pi

or Euler number:

> e

Sometimes even whole words work:

> speed of light
> speed of sound
> planck's constant
> boltzmann constant
> avogadro's number

or even this:

> number of horns on a unicorn
> once in a blue moon
> bakers dozen

The meaning of life | 24

A search engine this able will obviously know the meaning of life if you ask it exactly as it was asked in *A Hitchhiker's Guide to the Galaxy* by Douglas Adams:

the answer to life, the universe, and everything

You will get the answer from the novel: 42.

25 | Explanations from dictionaries and encyclopaedias

You encounter an unknown word and struggle your way to the nearest encyclopaedia. There's no need for that. Google understands the command define:, followed by a search string that Google searches for in dictionaries and encyclopaedias. Let's say you want to find out what the word "angst" means:

> define:angst

Or how the measure unit "Watt" is defined:

> define:watt

Maybe you don't know the meaning of an abbreviation:

> define:cpi

You can type in information about a person famous enough to appear in encyclopaedias. In this case, put the name and surname in quotation marks so that Google will search for this exact person and no one else.

> define:"rabindranath tagore"

What's the time? 26

A friend from San Francisco is waiting for your call. Are you wondering what time it is on the other side of the planet? Don't waste time counting on your fingers. Just type in the local time in command, followed by the name of the city:

> local time in san francisco

Google shows the local time of San Francisco. When abroad, you can always type in your home town. And if it's one of those mornings when you don't even know where you are, let alone what time it is, type in:

> local time

27 | What's the weather like?

Type in the weather command, followed by the name of a city. You will get data on the current state and a four-day forecast.

```
weather delhi
weather helsinki
```

Music | 28

You are searching for information about a musician or a band – something to do with music. If you start your search string with the music: command, Google will narrow down its hits to the field of music, which is no big deal, but it will also arrange them much more neatly:

```
music:"beatles"
```

For those of you searching for MP3 music files, check page 32.

Images for **music "the beatles"**

Videos for **music "the beatles"**

The Beatles - Come Together
4 min - 10 Apr 2008
SrisonS
www.youtube.com/watch?v=N8LZGQ4MkvQ

The Beatles - Rock & Roll **Music**
3 min - 19 Jun 2007
JohnPaulGeorgeRingo
www.youtube.com/wat v=TBiLhQpaUaM

The Beatles - You've Got to Hide Your Love Away
2 min - 6 Nov 2007
parlophone
www.youtube.com/watch?v=jz7IjXu0DfiQ

Beatles Radio: Solos, Covers, Biirthdays, News The Fab 4 and More!
Beatles Radio the **Music** of **the Beatles**, Solos, Covers, Biirthdays, News, The Fab 4 More! ... Picture of Book: Let's put **the Beatles** back together Again ...
www.beatlesradio.com/ - Cached - Similar

The Beatles LOVE | Las Vegas Show at The Mirage | Cirque du Soleil
With **The Beatles** LOVE, Cirque du Soleil celebrates the **musical** legacy of **The Beatles** through their timeless, original recordings.
www.cirquedusoleil.com/en/shows/love/default.aspx - Cached - Similar

iTunes - **Music** - **The Beatles**
Preview and download top **songs** and albums by **The Beatles** on the iTunes Store. **Songs** by

29 | Movies

Google has a special format for a music search, so there is no reason for movies to be neglected.
Use the film: command and type in the title of a movie, and you will get basic information, reviews, etc.

film:don

If you want to go for a movie, just type showtimes, followed by the name of a city, and it will give you the cinema programme for that city:

showtimes delhi

Easter eggs | 30

Sometimes Google programmers build in their web page a feature that's not really useful, they do it just to entertain themselves and mean for the user to stumble upon it. These kinds of jokes are called "Easter eggs". Some of the examples of constants on page 40 are Easter eggs.
Try typing this in and watch what happens to your screen:

Do a barrel roll

Do you want to know the meaning of the word "askew"? Type it in and look at the tilted screen:

Sometimes Google changes its logo; the most famous example was the Pac-Man game in May 2010 – a lot of users forgot their search and just played the game. You can still find it here:
http://www.google.com/pacman/

31 | Searching for flights

Would you like to fly from Delhi to Mumbai? You can type in abbreviations of airports with a space in between.

> del mum

In fact, you get enough hits even by typing in names of cities.

Maybe you would like to know when the boss's plane will be flying from Delhi to London. Simply type in the name of the air company and the number of the flight and you will get information on the departure and arrival times.

Birthdays and birthplaces | 32

You are making a project and need to know where a person was born. If the person is famous enough to be in an encyclopedia, Google will have the answer for you. Just use the birthplace of command.

```
birthplace of tagore
```

You can use the of command to find out quite a bit of information. Here are a few more examples:

```
birthday of tagore
king of bhutan
wife of henry viii
```

Go ahead and explore!

Google	birthday of tagore	🔍
Search	About 244,000 results (0.79 seconds)	
Everything	Best guess for Rabindranath Tagore Date of birth is **7 May, 1881**	
Images	Mentioned on at least 2 websites including wikipedia.org and calcuttaweb.com - Show sources - Feedback	

33 | Stocks

With the stock: command and the abbreviation of shares on the stock market you can easily obtain information on the exchange rate along with the charts.
GOOG is short for Google's shares:

```
stock:goog
```

Where's that country, anyway? | 34

You are reading about a certain country but at that moment you can't say for sure where it is on the map. The location of command might come in handy – Google will draw a map and highlight the country:

> location of ghana

Also:

> where is argentina

Google can also help you with the question: What's the flag of a country? Type in the flag of command and the name of a country, and Google will show you the flag:

> flag of ghana

35 | And where is this city?

Add the word map to the search string of a city or town, and Google will show you a map at the top of the hits:

map vellore

You can also inquire as follows:

where is vellore

Or, to be more exotic:

where is bali

The highest mountains | 36

You are listening to the radio and you hear a prize-winning question: which is the highest mountain in a certain country. For this purpose Google has a special command – highest point in. As long as the quiz composers don't find out about it, all the prizes are yours:

highest point in monaco

37 | Number of inhabitants in a country

The population command gives you a quick answer to the question: How many people are there in a certain country?

> population australia

Capitals | 38

If you are interested in the name of the capital of a certain country, use the capital of command:

```
capital of south africa
```

39 | **GDP**

This is something for the economists – information on gross domestic product. The English abbreviation is a part of the gdp command:

> GDP belgium

Radius of planets | 40

Obviously there are no set rules for creating commands at Google – each programmer decides to use a form of his choice. There are some commands with colons, but this one has an underline character (the one that was forced to the ground by gravity: _). The r_ command tells Google to search for the radius of a planet. That's how you find out what the radius of the Earth is:

```
r_earth
```

Some other examples where the command is followed by a planet, the Moon and the Sun:

```
r_mars
r_moon
r_sun
```

41 | Masses of planets

Similar to the r_ command that shows you the radius of a planet, you can use the m_ command (the letter m and an underline character, followed by the name) that gives you information on the mass. For the mass of the Earth:

```
m_earth
```

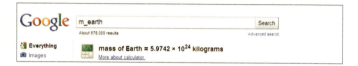

Some other examples where the command is followed by a planet, the Moon and the Sun:

```
r_mars
r_moon
m_sun
```

Advanced search

Google puts simple use first. Its website is very neatly organized: a search box and a key that starts the search, that's all. This is a proper **basic search**.
If you want more, you either need to remember Google's commands presented in the previous chapters or reach for a special form asking you what you want. By filling it in, you will indirectly use the right commands. The procedure is called an Advanced Search and you can enter it by clicking on a link to the right of the search box.

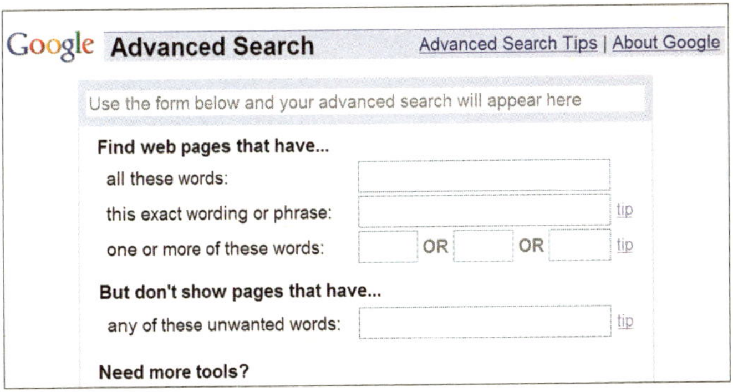

Google **Advanced Search**	Advanced Search Tips | About Google

Use the form below and your advanced search will appear here

Find web pages that have...
- all these words:
- this exact wording or phrase: tip
- one or more of these words: OR   OR   tip

But don't show pages that have...
- any of these unwanted words: tip

Need more tools?

42 | The advanced search form

Here is a box with commands and a search string that you compose by answering the questions underneath:

1

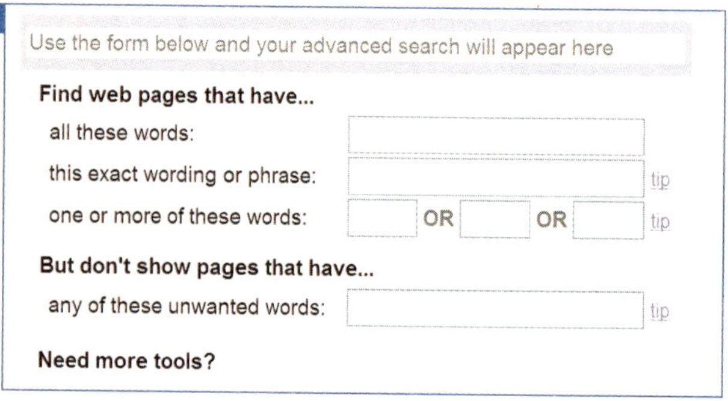

Use the form below and your advanced search will appear here

Find web pages that have...

all these words:

this exact wording or phrase: tip

one or more of these words: OR   OR   tip

But don't show pages that have...

any of these unwanted words: tip

Need more tools?

2

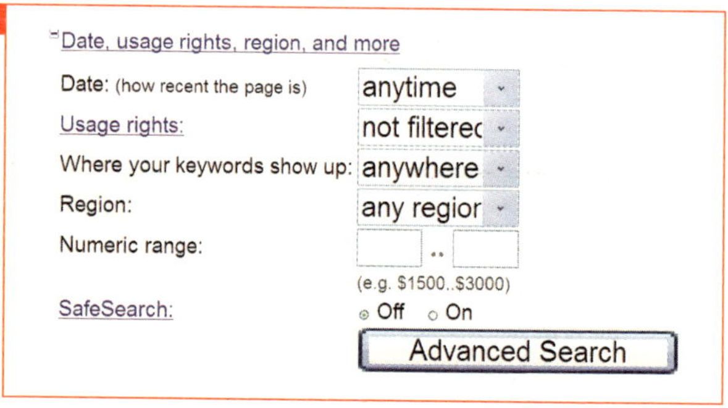

‾Date, usage rights, region, and more

Date: (how recent the page is)   anytime

Usage rights: not filtered

Where your keywords show up: anywhere

Region: any region

Numeric range: ..
(e.g. $1500..$3000)

SafeSearch: ⊙ Off   ○ On

Advanced Search

An exact string you are searching for (as if it were put in quotation marks, page 18).

Words you can't decide upon (the OR command, page 17).

Words you are looking for (as if they were typed in the basic search box, page 9).

Words you want to exclude from the hits (the − command, page 16).

The number of hits you want displayed.

Addresses of the pages or the domain endings you want Google to search (the same as the site: command, pages 20–21).

Languages of the pages you want Google to search.

Types of files you want Google to search (the same as the filetype: command, page 31).

How recent the page is – the date and time of the last update.

What kind of rights of use Google should consider; authors should protect their pages but sometimes don't.

Click this link to show additional questions.

Where the words you typed in are found (more commands, including allintitle:, page 26).

2 ⊖ Date, usage rights, numeric range, and more

Date: (how recent the page is)	anytime
Usage rights:	not filtered by license
Where your keywords show up:	anywhere in the page
Region:	any region
Numeric range:	..
	(e.g. $1500..$3000)
SafeSearch:	⊙ Off ○ On

Page-specific tools:

Find pages similar to the page:

Find pages that link to the page:

Topic-specific search engines from Google:

Google Book Search
Google Code Search New!
Google Scholar
Google News archive search

Apple Macintosh
BSD Unix
Linux
Microsoft

Which country Google should search in?

Searching for pages that are linked to the one given.

Links for a topic-specific search.

Searching for similar pages (the related: command, page 22).

Skip pornography or not?

Should Google search for numbers (the .. command, page 25)?

Translation from foreign languages

Google can translate from foreign languages, but let it be totally clear before you get your hopes sky-high: no, it can't substitute a human translator! And no, you can't use it for writing business letters or novels!
But should you come across a website in a language you don't understand, ask Google for help and you will get something that's funny at times, often unclear, but more or less useful enough for you to understand what the text is about. In short, it will be quick, comfortable and free.

You can find Google's translator by clicking the link "Language Tools" on the main page.

Here is the place to select which tool to choose, according to your interests:

Searching through websites in a foreign language | 43

First, you need to decide what you want. Let's say you want to search within Spanish sites for the word "car" but you don't know what it is called in Spanish.

Type in the word in the original language (i.e., car).

Chose the language of sites you want Google to search.

Click the key and Google will show you a list of hits and it will translate the titles of the sites.

44 | Translating text

Type in the text you need translated (you can also copy it from the clipboard by clicking Ctrl + C; if you don't know what I'm talking about, get yourself a handbook on the basics of computer science).

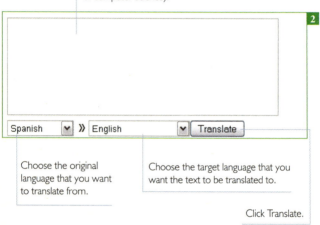

Choose the original language that you want to translate from.

Choose the target language that you want the text to be translated to.

Click Translate.

Translating websites | 45

Attention: Google will only translate the main text, leaving text on images (such as banners) in original language.

Type in the web address of the website you need translated; Google offers the http:// prefix

Translate a web page 3

http://

Spanish » English   [Translate]

Use the Google Interface in Your Language

Set the Google homepage, messages, and buttons to display in your selected language. Google currently offers the following interface languages:

- Afrikaans
- Akan
- Albanian
- Amharic
- Arabic
- Estonian
- Ewe
- Faroese
- Filipino
- Finnish
- Kazakh
- Kinyarwanda
- Kirundi
- Klingon
- Kongo

Choose the original language that you want to translate from.

Choose the target language that you want the text to be translated to.

Click Translate.

Google's topic-specific search

For searching special topics (such as images, videos, maps, news, products, etc.), Google has prepared special subsites that you can enter in two different ways:

Click the desired link on the basic search site.

Search Images Maps News Orkut Translate Gmail More ▾

There is no space for all Google's topics, though. Type in one of the web addresses from this chart in the toolbar.

Google Images	images.google.com	if searching for images (see also pages 71–75)
Google Videos	video.google.com/videohp	if searching for video clips
Google Maps	maps.google.com	if searching for maps (see also page 70)
Google News	news.google.com	within news
Google Product Search	google.com/shopping	comparison of prices
Google Books	books.google.com	within books

Google Scholar	scholar.google.co.in	within scientific articles
Google Finance	google.com/finance	financial information
Google Blog Search	google.com/blogsearch	searching through blogs (see also pages 76–79)
Google Alerts	google.com/alerts	alerts (see also pages 80–81)
Gmail	gmail.com	E-mail
Google Groups	groups.google.com	group discussions
Google Code	google.com/codesearch	code search for programmers
Google Patents	google.com/patents	American patents
You Tube	youtube.com	video sharing website
Google Calendar	calendar.google.com	calendar and organizer
Picasa	picasa.google.com	web album
Google Docs	docs.google.com	word processor and spreadsheet for sharing and collaborating online
Google Reader	reader.google.com	keeping up with your favorite websites
Google Sites	sites.google.com	creating a website
Google Chrome	google.com/chrome	browser
Google Translate	translate.google.com	free online language translation service (see also pages 63–67)
Google Mobile	google.com/mobile	access with phone
Google Plus	plus.google.com	social network

46 | Map search

Google has prepared a special subsite for searching maps and routes, which can be entered in two different ways:

In the title bar, type in the web address http://maps.google.co.in, or:

click the link Maps on the basic search site.

Image search | 47

For searching images, Google has prepared a special subsite that you can enter in two different ways:

In the title bar, type in the web address http://www.google.co.in/imghp, or:

click the link Images on the basic search site.

In this case, it is sufficient to type in "mouse", and Google will show you both the rodent as well as the computer accessory.

Searching within newspaper sources

On the subsite for the image search, you can use the special source: command that tells Google which source to go to for images. In the following example, it will search for the singer Caruso in the archives of the American Life magazine.

caruso source:life

The Life magazine is well-known for its photo archive and Google offers you some interesting insights.

Searching for faces

You are searching for images of a person and suddenly you realize that there are cities, cars and all sorts of things carrying the same name. Google can tell whether there is a face in an image or not.
You are searching for an image with the following keyword:

mercedes

You have only got cars, probably. Select "Face" on the scroll down menu. Cars disappear, only faces remain (well, perhaps there are some cars in the background).

Advanced Image Search

Each basic search has its advanced search (page 59), and so does the image search.

On the basic search site, click the link Images and then click the link Advanced Image Search.

An exact string you are searching for (as if they were put in quotation marks, page 18).

Words you can't decide upon (the OR command, page 17).

Words you are looking for (as if they were typed in the basic search box, page 9).

Words you want to exclude from your hits (the – command, page 16).

Images you want; yes, faces are among the choices.

The key that starts the search.

Google	**Advanced Image Search**		About Google
Find results	related to **all** of the words		Google Search
	related to the **exact phrase**		
	related to **any** of the words		
	not related to the words		
Content types	Return images that contain	⊙ any content ○ news content ○ faces ○ photo content ○ clip art ○ line drawings	
Size	Return images that are	Any size	
Exact size	Return images exactly the size	Width: Height:	Use my desktop size
Aspect ratio	Return images with an aspect ratio that is	Any aspect ratio	
Filetypes	Return only image files formatted as	any filetype	
Coloration	Return only images in	any colors	
Domain	Return images from the site or domain		
Usage Rights	Return images that are	not filtered by license	More info
SafeSearch	○ No filtering ⊙ Use moderate filtering ○ Use strict filtering		

Size of images

Should Google search only within one website; if so, which one (same as the site: command, pages 20–21)

Colour

Format of images

75

48 | Searching through blogs

Blogs are a special kind of website, designed mostly for daily publications of posts, opinions, etc. In short, these are public "diaries" that can be written by anyone.
If you are interested in public opinion on a certain topic, it's best if you search only within blogs. Google has prepared a special subsite which you can reach by:

typing the web address in the title bar of the browser: http://blogsearch.google.com, or:

clicking the link Blogs on the basic search site.

Searching within blog titles
You can search only within website titles (the allintitle: command, page 26) and you can also search only within blog titles. That's how you check if SRK has a blog under his name:

inblogtitle:srk

Searching within post titles
If you search for a post about Yash Chopra, you can type the name of the film director in quotation marks and search only within titles:

inposttitle:"yash chopra"

You can also search for a specific post within a blog. For example, if you want to find a post about Yash Chopra in the SRK blog:

inposttitle:"yash chopra" inblogtitle:king

Searching for authors

Some authors of blogs use their real names, others use pseudonyms. Google helps you search for these data, too. That's how you search for a Johnson, an author of a blog:

inpostauthor:johnson

Searching within a single blog

In this case, you need to know the web address of the blog, eg., www.shirky.com/weblog, which you type in after the blogurl: command:

```
blogurl:www.shirky.com/weblog
```

The command may come in handy when you combine different commands. Let's say the author wrote about the Amazon store:

```
amazon blogurl:www.shirky.com/weblog
```

To be more precise, let's say the author mentioned the name of this store in the title:

```
inposttitle:amazon blogurl:www.shirky.com/weblog
```

49 | Alerts

Some time ago, a friend of mine wrote a fan letter about a novel on her website. A few hours later, she received an e-letter in which the author was thanking her politely. She was so happy she almost cried. "The author reads my site. My site! Mine!"
Oh, well.
The author probably doesn't read her site, he just knows how to use Google Alerts.
You can tell the searcher to repeat a certain search and when a new site appears among the hits, Google sends you an e-mail.
This means the author wanted the searcher to alert him whenever his surname and the title of the novel appeared. When my friend wrote the letter, a new site appeared on the site index and the author received an e-mail.

In the title bar of the browser, type in the following web address: www.google.com/alerts.

Type in a search string, same as on the basic search site.

Choose a search type (for basic search don't change anything).

Choose how often the search should be carried out.

Type in your e-mail address to receive information about a new hit.

50 | What do others search for?

Whatever you may be searching for, whoever may be searching, Google saves all the information in its archive. Hmm, come to think of it – it's quite a frightening thought. However, you do have partial access to these archives.

In the title bar of your browser, type www.google.co.in/trends and press Enter.

How interesting is a certain site?

On the www.google.co.in/trends site you can type a web address into the search box, and you will get a graphic image of the visiting trend, along with scales of countries, cities and languages the searchers use. Let's say you type in this:

www.google.co.in

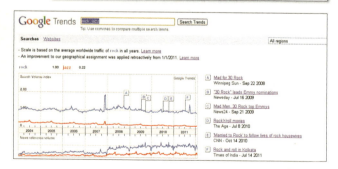

Attention: Statistics are only available for frequently visited sites!

Comparison of search words

On www.google.co.in/trends you can also compare how often two or more keywords are being searched for. Type in:

```
rock, jazz
```

You will get a chart showing frequency of searching by years.

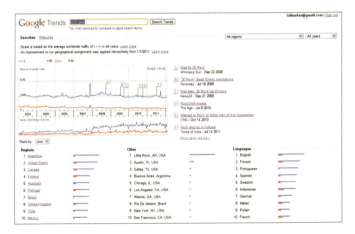

Attention: The words must be separated with commas.

At the time of going to press we checked every command to see if it was working. There is a chance Google has changed or even stop supporting some of them since. And there are definitely some new ones too. The best way to check is to google for them. :)

About the author

Miha Mazzini is the author of twenty-three books, published in eight languages. His stories can be found in more than a dozen anthologies in seven languages, including the *Bristol Short Story Prize Anthology, Volume 4* and *Pushcart Prize XXXVI*. Two of his screenplays have been produced as feature films, and he has written and directed five short films. He lives and works in Ljubljana, Slovenia.